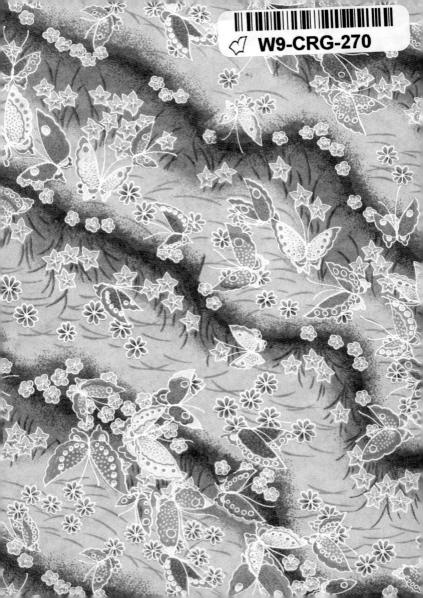

W9-CRG-270

A Baby Blessing

A Baby Blessing

BY WELLERAN POLTARNEES

LAUGHING ELEPHANT BOOKS • MMVII

COPYRIGHT © 1995, BLUE LANTERN STUDIO. ALL RIGHTS RESERVED.

THIRD PRINTING ~ SECOND EDITION. PRINTED IN CHINA THROUGH COLORCRAFT, LTD.

THIS TITLE IS ALSO AVAILABLE IN A LARGER EDITION

ISBN 1~59583~060~X

ISBN13 978~1~59583~060~9

LAUGHING ELEPHANT BOOKS

3645 INTERLAKE AVENUE NORTH, SEATTLE, 98103

WWW.LAUGHINGELEPHANT.COM

I here bless this baby,
newly arrived, wishing for it all the good
things I here invoke, and others beyond my
imaginings.

May the spirits of grace attend its coming,
and may angels guide its flowering.

3

*Let this child be held and warmed,
made secure in this strange new world.*

5

When this baby first opens its eyes,
may the face it first looks upon
be filled with love.

I pray that it be welcomed by many,
loved by many, and known by a myriad
of private and gentle names.

9

When this baby looks beyond
the faces of its family,
let it look upon a room where beauty reigns.
Let there be shapely toys waiting to be
touched into life, and a window
with a view of the world outside.

*I wish for this child to know early in life
the hugeness of trees, the cold kiss of
snowflakes and the softness of rain.*

THE FIRST SNOW.

May this small life be made rich with music.
Let there be songs on waking, happy songs at
play and gentle songs at night.

Let this baby's sleep be peaceful, and may it sail back each morning filled with the memory of sweet dreams.

17

May play fill this young life as it blossoms, so that it may come to enjoy solitude as much as shared joy.

19

I hope that there are many animal
companions, each teaching gentleness,
playfulness and kinship.

May this young body grow fully, move freely, breathe deeply and see clearly.

23

I hope, as this baby grows into childhood,
that those it meets praise it freely,
encouraging its fragile mystery to bloom
into radiant self.

25

When this child grows up and has children
of its own, let it never forget what it was like
to be first alive and richly welcomed.

Let those who share in this baby's growing
learn from its laughter and joy.

Picture Credits

FRONT COVER	JESSIE WILLCOX SMITH. MAGAZINE ILLUSTRATION (1918).
ENDPAPERS	FRENCH WALLPAPER (CIRCA 1925).
DEDICATION PAGE	M. FISCHEROVÁ-KVĚCHOVÁ. FROM *PAMÁTNIK NAŠEHO DĚTÁTKE* (1922).
FRONTISPIECE	S. BEATRICE PEARSE. MAGAZINE ILLUSTRATION (1917).
TITLE PAGES	(LEFT & RIGHT)
	MAGINEL WRIGHT BARNEY. MAGAZINE ADVERTISEMENT (1929).
COPYRIGHT PAGE	HONOR C. APPLETON. FROM *BLACKIE'S CHILDREN'S ANNUAL* (1917).
1	JOAQUIN SOROLLA. "THE MOTHER" (DETAIL) (1895).
2	CICELY MARY BARKER. POSTCARD (CIRCA 1926).
3	ARTHUR RACKHAM. FROM *THE SPRINGTIDE OF LIFE* (1918).
4	FREDERICK WILLIAM ELWELL. "THE FIRST BORN" (1913).
5	ANONYMOUS. MAGAZINE ILLUSTRATION (1922).
6	ANONYMOUS. PRINTED ILLUSTRATION (1922).
7	ANONYMOUS. FROM *THE HOME INVENTORY CALENDAR* (CIRCA 1900).
8	JOHN HENRY LORIMER. "SPRING MOONLIGHT" (CIRCA 1890).
9	ADA W. SHULZ. "MOTHERHOOD" (CIRCA 1925).
10	MARIE MADELEINE FRANC-NOHAIN. FROM *LE JOURNAL DE BÉBÉ* (1914).
11	ANNE ANDERSON. FROM *BABY'S RECORD* (1920).
12	BLANCHE FISHER WRIGHT. FROM *BABY'S JOURNAL* (1916).
13	HARRIETT M. BENNETT. FROM *WHEN ALL IS YOUNG* (CIRCA 1889).
14	JESSIE WILLCOX SMITH. FROM *THE JESSIE WILLCOX SMITH MOTHER GOOSE* (1914).
15	KATHARINE HAYWARD GREENLAND. FROM *BABY DEAR* (1908).
16	KATHARINE WIREMAN. FROM *HOW TO BRING UP A BABY* (1906).
17	JOHN GEORGE MEYER VON BREMEN. "THE NEW BABY" (1855).
18	ANONYMOUS. MAGAZINE ADVERTISEMENT (1928).
19	MAGINEL WRIGHT ENRIGHT. MAGAZINE ILLUSTRATION (1922).
20	RUTH MARY HALLOCK. FROM *STUDIES IN READING* (1924).
21	ARTHUR JOHN ELSLEY. "TEA TIME" (DETAIL) (1904).
22	ANNIE BENSON MÜLLER. MAGAZINE ADVERTISEMENT (1934).
23	S.L. RUNYON. PRINTED ILLUSTRATION (1908).
24	M. SAMMIE JACK. MAGAZINE ADVERTISEMENT (1920).
25	ANNIE BENSON MULLER. MAGAZINE ADVERTISEMENT (1934).
26	GEORGER VARIAN. "ST. NICHOLAS VOL. XXXVII PT. 1" (1910).
27	BERNARD POTHAST. MAGAZINE ILLUSTRATION (1925).
28	LORENTZ FROELICH. "BONSOIR PETIT PÈRE" (CIRCA 1873).
29	ANNIE BENSON MÜLLER. MAGAZINE ILLUSTRATION (1922).
30	ANONYMOUS. CALENDAR ILLUSTRATION (CIRCA 1920).
32	ROCKWELL KENT. MAGAZINE ADVERTISEMENT (1934).
33	THE REESES. MAGAZINE ADVERTISEMENT (1930).
BACK COVER	PHILIP BOILEAU. MAGAZINE ILLUSTRATION (1915).

THIS BOOK IS TYPSET IN POETICA
BOOK & COVER DESIGN BY SACHEVERELL DARLING AT BLUE LANTERN STUDIO.

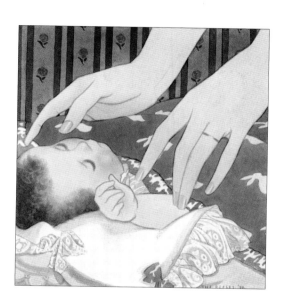

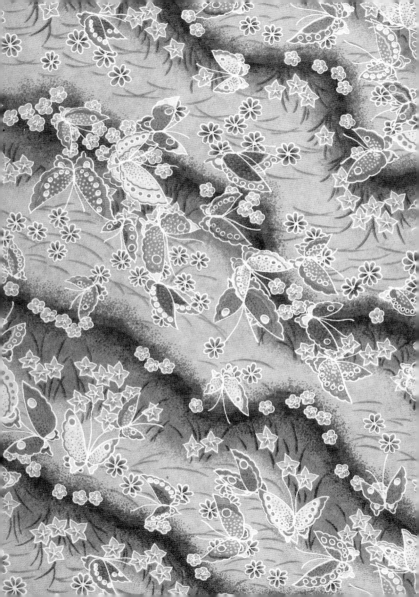